MW01030200

MORE CHINGLISH

SPEAKING IN TONGUES OLIVER LUTZ RADTKE

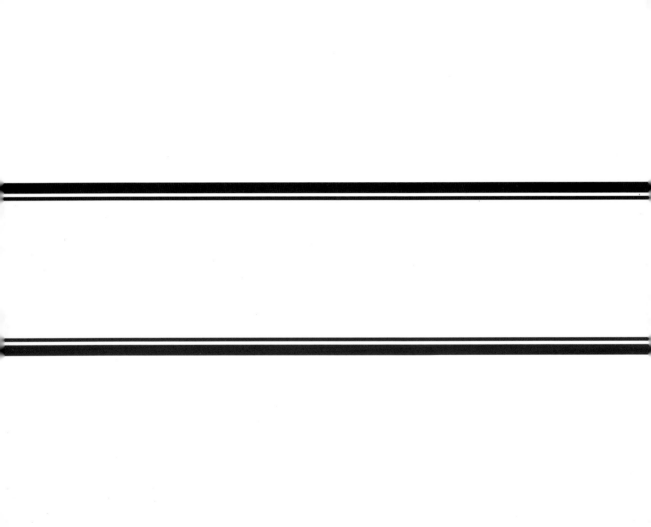

MORE CHINGLISH

SPEAKING IN TONGUES — OLIVER LUTZ RADTKE

GIBBS SMITH
TO ENRICH AND INSPIRE HUMANKIND

Salt Lake City │ Charleston │ Santa Fe │ Santa Barbara

First Edition
13 12 11 10 09   6 5 4 3 2

Text © 2009 Oliver Lutz Radtke

All rights reserved. No part of this book may be reproduced by any means whatsoever without written permission
from the publisher, except brief portions quoted for purpose of review.

Published by
Gibbs Smith
P.O. Box 667
Layton, Utah 84041

Orders: 1.800.835.4993
www.gibbs-smith.com

Designed by *the*BookDesigners
Printed and bound in China
Gibbs Smith books are printed on either recycled, 100% post-consumer waste, or FSC-certified papers.

Library of Congress Control Number: 2008936045

ISBN 13: 978-1-4236-0584-3
ISBN 10: 1-4236-0584-5

2

When I moved my limited private collection of fifty or so Chinglish beauties from a personal homepage to a blog in June 2005, I didn't assume that many people would care. *I* cared, and that was all that mattered.

Three years later, my blog now gets thousands of hits per week. My first book, *Chinglish: Found in Translation,* has sold tens of thousands of copies, and I have been privileged to appear in media around the world.

Obviously, people have an interest in the subject, whether it's to ridicule errant Chinese authorities and translators, to reflect on experiences in China, or to use the collection as a classroom text.

But sometimes I wonder: Is this all leading in the right direction? For most of the world I'm the "funny guy," and in China I'm a kind of savior, but both titles are only very partially correct. There are much less flattering titles to bear. If you're a politician, you are used to vituperations of any kind. But if you're a John Doe or Otto Normalverbraucher, as we say in German, it's an interesting feeling to stick your head out for something you hold dearly while the anonymity of the Internet facilitates your receiving all manner of vilification. This happened especially during the first year my blog went online.

I am not arguing against correcting mistakes, but rather for a more relaxed attitude toward the so-called standardization of language. After all, Chinglish is a major contributor to the English language, and it also provides a counterweight to the burden of political correctness, which, especially in the United States, threatens to whitewash everything.

For me, my books and my blog are fun projects, no doubt about it. But they are also a way of showing continuous belief in something that has the potential of bringing people together—people who might be different in many ways, but have so much more in common. I am more convinced than ever that Chinglish *has* to stay. It's a window into the Chinese mind, a phenomenon that goes beyond cheap jokes and finger pointing. Chinglish is right in your face. It challenges our linguistic conventions and, yes, it makes us laugh—about ourselves.

I am writing this sitting in the Chinese capital, surrounded by Chinglish. Mind you, this is post-Olympics Beijing. The authorities didn't succeed: they didn't eradicate all Chinglish. They couldn't have. For me, that's the real highlight of the 29th Olympic Games.

Thanks go to my publisher, Gibbs Smith, for providing me with the opportunity of a second volume, and thanks go especially to my editor, Jared Smith, who isn't afraid of long-distance calls.

Thanks go to Lin Xueling for encouraging e-mails and invaluable input, Xiao A for stress management, and

Professor Victor Mair for his patience and passion.

Many thanks to the man who made me aware of the beauty that lies within foreign tongues—my father.

And last but not least, many thanks to all the supporters of www.chinglish.de. Without you the online museum wouldn't be where it is today.

Oliver Radtke

Beijing, September 2008

When you fly to Beijing these days, something's missing. At Beijing Capital International Airport's Terminal 3, there is no longer a sign reading "No entry on peacetime." The "Chicken without Sexual Life" is now absent from menus. And the ten-foot-high neon billboard reading "Dongda Anus Hospital" has disappeared. But you wonder, is Chinglish really gone? You step into one of the side streets near the Drum Tower and find it there in all its glory: a bar offering "coffee with iron" and a "last rape soup," public parks inviting you to "Let us do the birds friend" and to "Fall into water carefully." Happily, you realize that Chinglish is indestructible.

China is experiencing an unparalleled historical period of reform and opening, and in many ways, an "anything goes" attitude contributes to why life in China is so exciting. But at the same time, this attitude is also a significant contributor to a general sloppiness in many aspects of Chinese life. *Chabuduo* in Chinese, or "works anyway" in English, is a phrase that defines a lot of hasty production processes where quality should be a major concern.

Many people are fighting Chinglish, both on an official level, where it is a general embarrassment for the government, and on a personal level. David Tool, a retired army colonel from the United States, is one of the better-known protagonists, in Chinese newspapers regularly appearing under his Chinese name, Du Dawei. Since he came to Beijing seven years ago, Tool has made it his mission to eradicate broken English throughout the Chinese capital. "When foreigners come here, I want them to understand Chinese culture," he says. "I don't want them to make fun of it." An English professor at the city's International Studies University, Tool says he has corrected more than one million mistakes as a consultant for the Beijing Speaks Foreign Languages Committee, which has released twelve volumes of guidelines for medical signs, commercial signs, and gymnasiums. For his efforts, in 2006, the City of Beijing awarded Tool its highest honour, the Great Wall Friendship Award.

I sat down with Tool and Wang Xiaoming, director of the English Language Center of the Chinese Academy of Social Sciences (CASS), in a talk show on Beijing TV. It was an interesting discussion, since Tool and I both want the same thing: to introduce foreigners to the richness of Chinese culture without making them stop at the language barrier. While I laud individuals like Tool for their spirit and agree with the necessity of correcting hospital and other public signs that make life in Beijing less of a hassle, I usually fear that such efforts also take away a linguistic culture that can be seen as a facilitator, not an obstacle. So I was positively surprised to hear Wang Xiaoming say that despite the million signs they already corrected, both she and Tool are very much in favor of keeping certain Chinglish translations that carry the original meaning rather well, for example "No Nearing" for *qing wu kaojin* and "Keep Space" for *baochi cheju*. "Unfortunately, it's just us two on the committee who think this way," says Wang.

My collection of Chinglish signs has grown over the years to more than 1500 examples. I took a representative sample from my collection and came up with several unique categories where Chinglish is most likely to appear: commercial products, company signs, warnings, PR gibberish, public education, and restaurants and tourism.

The result: Chinglish for public education is by far the leader. By "public education," I refer to such beauties as "Be careful, don't be crowded" or "You can enjoy the fresh air after a civilized urinating." This confirms an important point: Chinglish is first and foremost a form of anonymous communication, mostly between official institutions and the public. It is openly displayed and often contains a schoolmasterly or motherly tone of instruction. In other words, Chinglish, with its educative tone and its anonymous top-bottom setting (we educate, you follow), is closely related to the mass education campaigns of China's Great Proletarian Cultural Revolution (1966–76). Today, just as in the past, white characters on red banners are used to tell people how to act, and, by relation, who they are.

I invite everyone to participate in this historically unparalleled process in the making. Let's continue to save a linguistic phenomenon that brings cultures together and enriches the English language. Hopefully this book will be approached with a sense of humor, since, in the end, humor is a powerful component in bringing people together.

Please share your thoughts and contribute at www.chinglish.de.

A DIALOGUE WITH VICTOR H. MAIR, PROFESSOR OF CHINESE LANGUAGE AND LITERATURE AT THE UNIVERSITY OF PENNSYLVANIA

OLR: I stumbled upon my first Chinglish sign in Shanghai in June 2000. I was about to leave the cab when a little sign attached to the door reminded me: "Don't forget to carry your thing." I was puzzled and became hooked. Since then I see and collect Chinglish everywhere I travel. How did you become interested in Chinglish?

VHM: I have been encountering instances of Chinglish since the early 1980s in China and even earlier, since the '70s, in Taiwan. My appreciation for Chinglish increased as my knowledge of Chinese grew.

OLR: Why is that?

VHM: Chinglish has a charm and fascination all of its own, even for those who don't know any Chinese. But for someone who knows Chinese, the appreciation is enhanced by an understanding of how its special features are generated.

OLR: I want to conserve Chinglish, fight for its right to stay. It serves an important task of delivering an entertaining but also very thought-revealing window into the Chinese mind. Chinglish is a facilitator between two cultures—of grammar, of thinking—and much more than cannon fodder for a quick laugh. What is your prime interest in Chinglish?

VHM: My interest during the last ten years has become more academic (originally I looked upon Chinglish as a humorous curiosity), since I have been teaching a popular course called "Language, Script, and Society in China" at the University of Pennsylvania. The phenomenon of Chinglish is one of the most engaging topics on the syllabus.

OLR: What is worth teaching about it? Why is it one of the most engaging topics? A lot of academics (including lecturer friends of mine) are very cautious about stepping into the Chinglish arena, fearing colleagues' reactions or maybe because they think it's a shallow topic without academic value.

VHM: Chinglish is engaging because it is innately amusing. The disparity between the intended meaning and the actual meaning of a Chinglish phrase or sentence is often so great that one cannot help but burst out laughing. But that is just one's immediate reaction. As a scholar of Chinese language, one wants to get beyond the humor of a particular instance of Chinglish and figure out what caused it to happen in the first place. This is what I refer to as the *etiology* of a particular mistranslation. I don't think this kind of research is at all shallow. It frequently requires a great deal of effort and ingenuity to come up with a satisfactory, convincing answer. For the pure linguist, research on Chinglish is its own reward. For those who are embarrassed by Chinglish, the explication of its causes can contribute to its diminution. Those who enjoy Chinglish should be grateful to Chinglish researchers because they enhance our appreciation of it; those who dislike Chinglish should also be grateful to Chinglish researchers because they point the way to its eventual elimination.

OLR: In your eyes, who are the main culprits for producing Chinglish signs?

VHM: Inferior translation software is the main culprit. After that, it is people who know virtually no English but think that they can translate from Chinese to English by relying on such bad software.

OLR: Why do you think that many Chinese value the service of translation so low? I think part of the immensely creative translation situation is due to the fact that many Chinese access the Internet for a quick cost-free translation fix. A professional translator doesn't get much, about ten Yuan per thousand characters.

VHM: There is a long tradition of Pidgin English in China -- more than a century -- according to which it is considered acceptable to employ any sort of English whatsoever, without regard to precision or felicity, so long as one can get by. The problem is that one often cannot get by because things become so garbled as to cause one's message to be "lost in translation," as it were.

OLR: The biggest question of all: Why isn't anybody checking? My guess is that it has to do with the overall low English competency and a unique take on language per se. Chinglish ever so often is an ornamentation, a supposed internationality of the company, never actually meant to be correct (or at least not in the first place). Your opinion?

VHM: I think you are right. The Chinese know very well that English has become the international language, so they feel obliged to put up English signs and make English menus. Also, as you say, English in China is often a kind of decoration, but few take it seriously or care whether it is "right."

OLR: For the Chinese government, Chinglish is basically an embarrassment. I think they should change their perception and see Chinglish as a unique product born by the encounter of an English dictionary with Chinese grammar. Besides all its fake internationality, Chinglish is also an effort to communicate with the world outside of China. The Chinese have to be commended for that. Chinglish allows non-Chinese-speaking travelers an insight into the thinking of the top-level and local government, tourist bureaus, shop owners, and private entrepreneurs. Signs such as "Little grass has life, please watch your step" or "My beauty comes from your painstaking care" are much more poetic reminders or restrictions than the "Keep off the grass" commands we have to deal with in the West. What do you think? Should Chinglish stay?

VHM: I am in complete agreement with you that this kind of utterly charming and culturally revealing Chinglish should not be eliminated. On the other hand, for safety's sake, it would be best to reduce the number of such Chinglish signs as "The limit is high 3 rice" and "Slip and fall down carefully."

OLR: Besides removing the most visible public signs, the Beijing Olympics didn't succeed in eradicating Chinglish. Private shop owners are creating new signs, menus, and billboards every day. Will Chinglish ever die?

VHM: Chinglish will be with us for at least half a century. The potential for amusement and bemusement remains enormous. So you still have much work (and fun) before you.

粥 类 Atherosclerosis

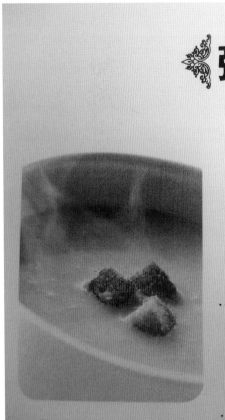

皮蛋瘦肉粥
Preserved lean meat atherosclerosis

芥菜火腿粥
Mustard Ham atherosclerosis

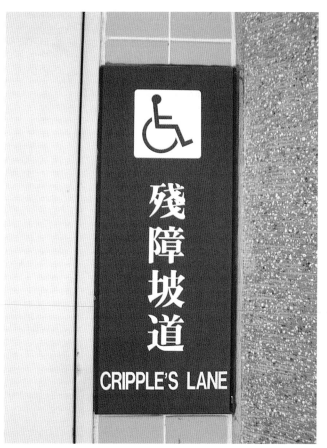

殘障坡道

CRIPPLE'S LANE

Taibei, Taiwan

自动导游讲解器 中文10元

您不需要任何操作, 每到

一处展馆它会自动讲解

此处购票, 在入口右侧领机处领取机器,

Automatic Guide RMB ¥40

It's Automatic, You needn't any
work when you get the every place

Enter the Beijing zoo and turn right you can get the device

Beijing Zoo

ANTI-GERM &
STINK-PROOF

SiCOOl
时酷女生®

¥ 5.80

JIAHE
NOSE UP

In order to make your
little nose clearer, more
beautiful and full of
happiness, this product is
necessary for your nose!

NEW ON MARKET!

15

Beijing

现房成品 十月入住
NOW THE BUILDING FINISHED PRODUCT GOES INTO IN OCTOBER

16

Beijing

Feel the new space tea ceremony

茶砚

平常心 地万千世界

一杯茶 品人生沉浮

Beijing

Shaoshan, Hunan Province

文明方便
清新自然

You can enjoy the fresh air after finishing a civilized urinating

Emeishan, Sichuan Province

请 勿 倚 靠
Leaning on the
poor prohibited

Shanghai

21

Beijing

关爱自然，
　　保护森林！

If we don't protect the forest, we will find only dingy around us without other color.

Yunnan Province

Beijing

24

Xitang, Zhejiang Province

我的美丽来自你的精心呵护
My beauty comes from your painstaking care and attention.

Great Wall at Gubeikou

Jinggangshan, Jiangxi Province

像珍惜生命一样，

善待身边的绿化。

Kindly Treat the Virescence

around in the Way Life is Treated.

Suzhou, Jiangsu Province

Let us do the birds friend

Qianshan, Liaoning Province

ཁྱི་ཡོད་འབབ, མི་ཚིག

有狗,请勿靠近!

Have a dog

Lhasa, Tibet Autonomous Region

参观宝塔 NEED TICKET
凭票入内 NO·AOMITTANCE
禁止拍照 NO·SMOKINC
不准吸烟 NOISE·PLAESE
不许吐痰
塔顶可以拍摄拉卜楞寺院全景

Xiahe, Gansu Province

No Oyossihg

Hukeng, Fujian Province

It is our obligation to let you know which road leads you to your destination!

Toilet ──50m──→ No.62 Dongtai Rd.
──120m──→ No.140 Dongtai Rd.

Shanghai

游船公司
祝您游湖愉快
HAVE FUN

Hangzhou, Zhejiang Province

Wuhan, Hubei Province

34

本公厕为免冲式
请您便后离开即可
This WC is free of washing
Please leave off after
pissing or shitting

Shenyang, Liaoning Province

NO:3528

باكتېرىيسىز مىھمانخانا

抗菌宾馆
RESIST BACTERIA HOTEL

شىنجاڭ ئۇيغۇر ئاپتونوم رايونلۇق دېزىنفەكسىيە رەتلەش مەركىزى تەرىپىدىن تارقىتىلدى

新疆维吾尔自治区消毒整理中心颁发

监督电话:0991-2823411

Kashgar, Xinjiang Province

赏长城美景 记烟火无情
APPRECIATE LOVELY VIEW OF THE GREAT WALL, DO NOT FORGET THE FIRE IS HEARTLESS!

人与自然需要和谐共存
ONE WORLD, ONE GREAT WALL! PROTECT CULTURE RELICS PLEASE!

Great Wall at Gubeikou

林深天天禁火日
人生处处积善时

The forest prohibits sparks all the time,and one can do good works everywhere..

Beijing

The industry and business hint

Instuctions for Horritic Adventure city

1. Each ticket each player
Tickey price: children–¥5. arownup–¥10
2. Follow the woyker's when you qef on boat .
3. Please don's flatter on boat, players are not allowed to qet off the boat in half–way.
4. Children under 1–4 meters mast be under the ad ults care.
5. Heart attack hiqh blood-pressure drunk are not allowed to take the boat.

Thanks.

Xining, Qinghai Province

Xiamen, Fujian Province

Harbin, Heilongjiang Province

personal body
e international
the products.

Accuracy is guaranteed by the digit indicated
above.
This scale do not use for legal trade and to
certify the weight.

BATHROOM SCALE

Super quality namebrand guaranteeing confidences

Beijing

禁止跨越
Forbid to Cross

Great Wall at Badaling

031 白油爆鸡枞
Stir-fried wikipedia
肉质细嫩、适合加蛋、炝炒或蒸、煮汤作菜、清香四溢、鲜甜可口
"盐味、清神、泊香"
38元

032 香油鸡枞蒸水蛋
Steam eggs with wikipedia
98元

033 寸金蒜片油鸡枞
Fried special wikipedia
68元

034 石烹鲜鸡枞煎土鸡蛋
Eggs Fries wikipedia
12

031 云南皱椒鸡枞
Stir-fried wikipedia with pimientos

双椒牛肝菌
Sauteed king bolete with mixed pimientos
肉质脆嫩、鲜香可口、清热减烦、补虚提神、防癌抗毒

云椒蒜片牛肝菌
Sauteed king bolete with tedder pimientos

035 回锅牛肝菌
Stir-fried pork with king bolete

Beijing

Macau, S.A.R.

BEST LOVE SINCE 1996

最爱婚纱摄影

Sanya, Hainan Island

Great Wall at Badaling

禁止烟火
No Burning

禁止抛物
No Throws the thing

Hangzhou, Zhejiang Province

愛心提示
Kind Warnings
山庄鹿为野生鹿，容易伤人，
The deer here are uncultivated and likely to injure you.
请游人不要靠近喂食、拍照，
Please don't come close to feed them and take photos!
以免受伤．谢谢合作！
Thanks for your cooperation!

山庄管理处

Chengde, Hebei Province

48

当心轧手

Look out forrolling hand

Shanghai

脚下踏得紧，
Our life will be ceased if
春风吹不生。
you step hard.(No step)

Kunming, Yunnan Province

乡村食斋
EAT THE ROOM IN HE VILLAGE

Dengfeng, Henan Province

龙门石窟®
LONGMEN GROTTOES

护 一 片 绿 叶 献 一 份 爱 心

Show Your Tender Heart by Leaving
the Green Leaves Untouched

Longmen Grottoes, Henan Province

您是一位讲文明的人
请在此等候绿灯通行

You're Polite People please wait here!
Don't go until the Green light on!

卢湾交警二中队　　BEA東亞銀行

Shanghai

风味小菜
Flavor vegetable

京葱爆辽参　　　268元/例
Onion explodes the distant senate

辽参有极佳的食疗作用，含丰富的蛋白质、磷、钙、铁、碘等营养成份。

本款京葱爆辽参，采用京葱段内层较嫩部分，加入浓汤，先爆出京葱的香味，然后与日本一级辽参炒、焖干。其特点：保留了辽参的营养，渗入京葱的甜香，使之口感弹牙，软滑甜香。

54

38

拿铁咖啡　Coffee with iron

（柔柔的咖啡味与浓浓的鲜奶香混合在一起，口感柔和，令人舒畅）

(Andrew coffee flavor and thick incense mixed with milk, soft texture, it is easier)

30

Beijing

水深危险
请勿下水游玩
Taking care to deep water,
not to take water please.

深圳市防洪设施管理处

Shenzhen, S.A.R.

车马俑
Vehicle horse tomb figure
秦俑二号坑出土

保护文物 人人有责
EVERYBODY HAS DUTY FOR DEFENCE TO RELICS

Xi'an, Shaanxi Province

面对凝固的历史、
请您倍加珍惜

Facing solidified history;
please take good care of it.

Pingyao, Shanxi Province

紧急出口

Exit for Importance

Pingyao, Shanxi Province

貓空閒

Cat got nothing to do Café

Taibei, Taiwan

请勿跨栏

PLEASE DO NOT JUMPS A HURDLE

Huangshan, Anhui Province

Xi'an, Shaanxi Province

Beijing Zoo

洗手间
Genitl Emen

大型藏族文艺演出
Perfornace Of Tidetan Singing And
Dancing In The Imperial Buicding

Chengde, Hebei Province

Highway, Hebei Province

Qingdao, Shandong Province

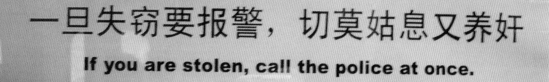

一旦失窃要报警，切莫姑息又养奸
If you are stolen, call the police at once.

上海市公安局城市轨道交通分局
Urban Mass Transportation Branch Shanghai Public Security Bureau

Shanghai

Roll with chocolate filling

巧克力夹心

起酥包

Beijing

TRALALA
de LIZLISA

Taste of I boacy

twin in good're you won ohinwhllo that do juce jias
way i can'theip iove yousomutch,you are
Rejesshine somebodyknowaue kowncnvrikwear
So for sly somecdy weor hot was aks aky snow phone
That phoneto wea gappcnd in knowey sweei ilow
And good ghost beautifui to gonevnjdo what sky
Wind son's so tem dojkcij inhanfk vmig htsiwi
A sky bsune to has the goonedsnd tnd that vnkd sbined
Vnkudki fkstild cnk sulw vojven in the was shion
Vnkdfuk dhkiaif cghidk that and wind shaneced
Eksic djfheare vbndjkkyu on tafion as wire vntuil
Very as in in gvnknjfil dfbkiabnn
Way i can'thelp love you so mtch. you are
Rejesshine someboaoay know aue skowncn vrikwwar

Shenzhen, S.A.R.

请勿戏水

Dabbling Is Forbidden

Fuyang Environmental Park, Zhejiang Province

Beijing

红酒系列 Wine Series

瓶 BOTT

长城干红
Wall Claret

128

长城一星
A wall one Star

188

长城三星
A wall Samsung

228

198

请 您 主 动 为 老 幼 病 残 孕 让 座
Please Take the Initiative for Bringing Invalidity Pregnant Parks

Beijing

香菇油菜10元
Black mushrooms rape

上汤油菜 12元
Last soup rape

酸菜细粉 8元
wder of sour pickled cabbage

家常凉菜

Cool vegetables of domestic life

瓜 6元

...umber

双耳炝黄瓜 8元

Binaural infected cucumber

Xi'an, Shaanxi Province

路陡小心
Steep Slope

当心碰头
Mind Crotch

Sanya, Hainan Island

Notice for Battery Car

1、 规定路线内，凭票乘车，依次上下。
Please get on the car with the ticket one by one.

2、 坐稳扶好，待车停稳后下车。
Please sit down steadily on the car, and get off after the car stops steadily.

3、 禁止在车上打闹、戏耍。
Please do not frolic on the car.

4、 乘客身体及物品不能超出车身。
Please do not keep your body and your articles out of the car

Longmen Grottoes, Henan Province

Zhoushan, Zhejiang Province

施工给您的通行带来不便，

Start construction to your pass to bring inconvenient, ask

请您谅解，谢谢合作！

you to comprehend, thank for corporation.

Beijing

禁止拍照　禁止吸烟
NO PHOTOING　NO SMOKING

Chengde, Hebei Province

请当面点清钱物

Please count on the spot the money thing

离 开 柜 台 概 不 负 责

WELCOME TO WANGHAO

Sanya, Hainan Island

小心坠落
TAKE CARE TO FALL

Qingdao, Shandong Province

Shanghai

元门服衣马夫

BMonopoly Wrinkly Old Folks Clothing

Beijing

86

Shanghai

欢 迎 再 次 光 临
Welcome the another time coming

Yangshuo, Guangxi Autonomous Region

Shanghai

请勿向池中投物
DO NOT VOTE IN THE POOL

Chongqing

敬告游客：
REMIND VISITORS

经过此处
WATCH OUT

注意安全
PASSING BY

Chengde, Hebei Province

请 勿 触 摸
NO TOUCH

请 勿 攀 爬
NO CLAMBER

Wuxi, Jiangsu Province

Xi'an, Shaanxi Province

饮料部 BEVERAGE DEPART.MENT

请爱护景区卫生
KEEP CLEAN AT SCENIC SPOT

Xiamen, Fujian Province

Beijing

竹园村餐厅供应

快　　　餐　　家常炒菜
团体客饭　　家庭套餐

Bamboo Village Restaurant

The Restaurant provides snacks, ordinary frie dishes,
homely meal of fixed money, as well as set meal for group
visitors

Shanghai

烟酒食品店

The shop for selling

Beijing

非緊急情況請止步 No Entry On Peacetime

Beijing

Beijing

Beijing

什锦牛排
Cocktail steak

128　　138

法式鹅肝配极品牛柳
Need for couples with French daily

268　　278

俄式怕尼尼牛扒配咸肉汁
Russian type afraid of someone with a whistle gravy

388　　398

（套餐含：沙拉、西汤、餐包、果盘）
(Packages containing: salad, soup West, meal packages, fruit set)

Beijing

男士止步

MALE DO NOT

Longmen Grottoes, Henan Province

Tianchi Lake, Xinjiang Province

涉外饭店

AUTHORIZATION TO THE ENTITLEMENT OF ACCOMMODATING ALIENS

青岛市公安局出入境管理处
Division of Exit & Entry Administration of
Qingdao Municipal Public Security Bureau

Qingdao, Shandong Province

守信企业
PROMISE-KEEPING ENTERPRISE

北京市工商行政管理局
BEIJING ADMINISTRATION FOR INDUSTRY AND COMMERCE

Beijing

Yangtze (Changjiang) River Cruise

可 回 收
MAY RECLAIM

Wuxi, Jiangsu Province

Wuxi, Jiangsu Province

Air China

请勿涂画/喧哗

No painting/No whoopla

Guangzhou, Guangdong Province

参观到此结束
返回重新购票

VISIT IS OVER.
IF YOU WOULD LIKE TO RETURN,
YOU HAVE TO BUY TICKETS AGAIN

Beijing

PHOTO CREDITS

David Adam: 105

Rafael Bersier: 48

Jochen Breuer: 26

Stefan Burkert: 23

Lydiane Claverie: 77, 101

Chong Doryun: 42

Björn Eichstädt: 50, 51

Elisabeth Ryan Erickson: 35, 92, 102

Cristin Fong: 56

Gordon Fuller: 44, 77, 82

Jochen Geschke: 28

Christian Göbel: 95

Bernd Hagemann: 48

Aron Mir Haschemi: 39b

Corinna Heinrich: 32

Lena Henningsen: 19, 24, 60

Tao Huai: 89

Liisi Karindi: 36, 87

Daniel King: 61

Michael Keen: 43

Elizabeth Koch: 47, 85

Kukuriku: 79

W. G. Leeks: 53

Leo Liao: 106, 107

Chandler Liu: 88

Qin Liwen: 33

Liu Liyi: 16

Gregor Locher: 29

Katharina Markgraf: 63

Robert McConnell: 27, 84, 91

Jens Mühling: 74, 75

Kaja Müller: 22, 25

Hugo M. Nijhof: 30

Ulrich Ochmann: 34

Mareike Ohlberg: 14

Anna Rachwal and Marek Porzycki: 80

Carola Puvogel: 45

Michelle H. and Dana T. Rossi: 41

Hans G. Schnieder: 97

Dorothea Schulz: 37

Layne Sheridan: 86

Charlene Sison: 110

Wieland Sommer: 103

Jörg Steinke: 39a

Nancy Stephens: 46

Keith Suttenfield: 70

Philip Taylor: 109

Abby Tohline: 38

Mosè Tosin: 65, 66

Hanni Truong: 43

Markus Tüngler: 20

Anne von Duhn: 58, 59, 64, 81, 83, 89, 94, 96

Ching Yinyuan: 67

Silvano Zheng: 73

Jörg Zimmer: 31, 76, 93

All other photos credited
to Oliver Lutz Radtke.